UNCLE SAM AND OLD GLORY

Uncle Sam and Old Glory

Symbols of America

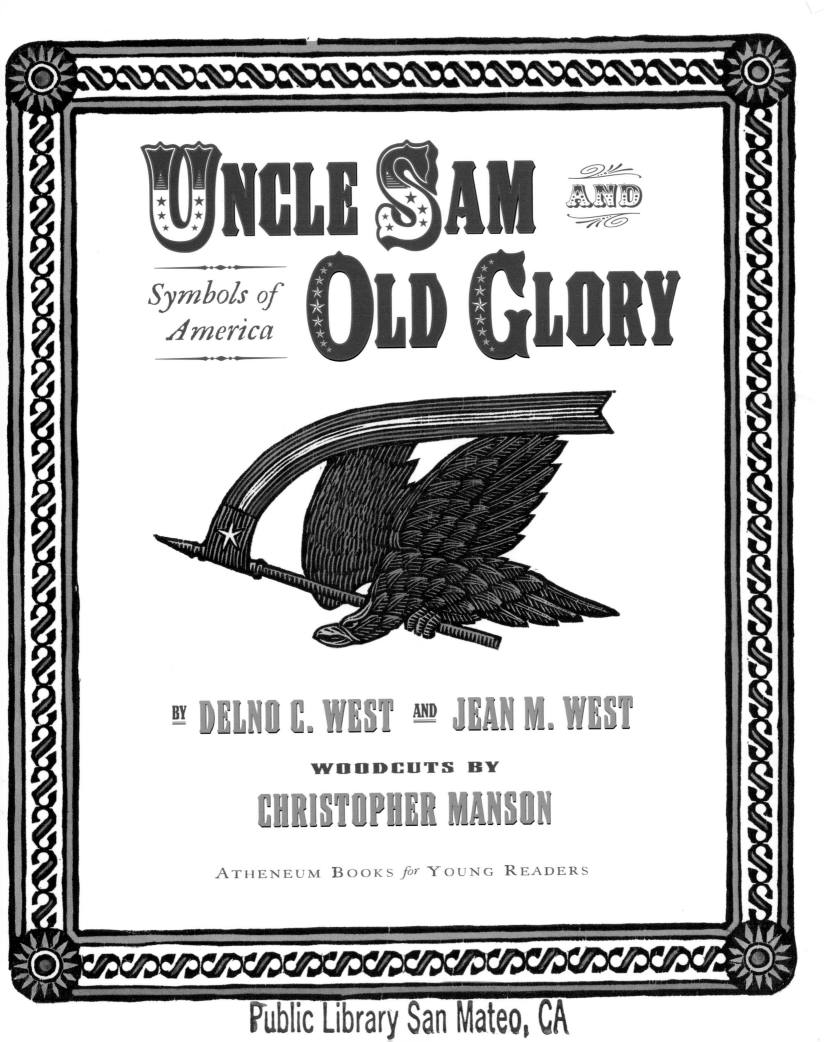

BY DELNO C. WEST AND JEAN M. WEST

WOODCUTS BY

CHRISTOPHER MANSON

ATHENEUM BOOKS for YOUNG READERS

THIS BOOK IS DEDICATED TO OUR
NEWEST GRANDCHILDREN:
WILLIAM LEE WEST
and
ALEXANDRA LYNN MARIE STROMING
—D. C. W. and J. M. W.

FOR PATRICIA
—C. M.

✶

Friendly, generous, loving, humorous, kind, and devoted
are all words to describe Dr. Delno C. West. He will be missed by many,
but especially by his wife, children, and grandchildren.   —J. M. W.

✶

Atheneum Books for Young Readers
An imprint of Simon & Schuster Children's Publishing Division
1230 Avenue of the Americas
New York, New York 10020

Text copyright © 2000 by Delno C. West and Jean M. West
Illustrations copyright © 2000 by Christopher Manson

Book design by Michael Nelson

The text of this book is set in Regula
The illustrations were cut in wood, printed, and painted by Christopher Manson

Printed in Hong Kong
2 4 6 8 10 9 7 5 3 1

Library of Congress Cataloging-in-Publication Data
West, Delno C., 1936-1999
Uncle Sam and Old Glory: Symbols of America / by Delno C. West and Jean M. West;
illustrated by Christopher Manson.—1st ed.
p. cm.
Summary: Presents the backgrounds of such American symbols as Uncle Sam and the Liberty Bell.
ISBN 0-689-82043-7
1. Emblems, National—United States—Juvenile literature. [1. Emblems, National.]
I. West, Jean M. II. Manson, Christopher, ill. III. Title.
JC346.W47   2000   929.9'2'0973—dc21   98-22268

FIRST
EDITION

CONTENTS

INTRODUCTION

From Smokey the Bear to the Statue of Liberty, we use symbols to express our ideas about ourselves as Americans. Our symbols come in many different forms: objects such as the log cabin and the *Mayflower,* animals like the bald eagle and the buffalo, the characters of the Pilgrim and the cowboy, even songs like "Yankee Doodle." These symbols give us a sense of community and show other countries some of the things that are important about America: freedom, democracy, and a spirit of optimism. When we wave miniature flags in a parade on the Fourth of July or look at the deep crack in the Liberty Bell, sometimes we feel strong emotions because they remind us of these values.

Symbols also have interesting stories behind them. Did you know that a long time ago, the main symbol for America was an Indian maiden? Or that the cartoon character of Uncle Sam began as a stamp on pieces of meat? Imagine if our national bird had been declared a turkey, as some people wanted? And you probably always wondered what the word "macaroni" was doing in the song "Yankee Doodle," but we bet you never guessed that it was a popular hairstyle in London in the 1750s.

In the following pages, we will explore where our symbols came from, what they mean, and how they have come to identify us as Americans to the rest of the world.

UNCLE SAM AND OLD GLORY

The AMERICAN FLAG

~⭐~

EVERY MORNING, MILLIONS OF CHILDREN IN CLASSROOMS across America stand with their hands over their hearts and say these words: "I pledge allegiance to the flag of the United States of America, and to the Republic for which it stands, one nation under God, indivisible, with liberty and justice for all." They address these words to the American flag, which is sometimes called the "Stars and Stripes," "Old Glory," or the "Star-Spangled Banner."

In July 1775, George Washington, the new commander of the Continental Army, thought a special flag should be made to represent all the colonies who were rebelling against the British government. So the Continental Congress, the government at the time, came up with a design and approved it on June 14, 1777. Most people think that General Washington then asked a Philadelphia seamstress named Betsy Ross to sew the first flag, but no one really knows if this is true.

The red, white, and blue colors and the stars and stripes are symbols of the American spirit. White stands for liberty, red for courage, and blue symbolizes loyalty. Every aspect of the flag's design stands for an important idea, too. The thirteen red and white stripes represent the original thirteen colonies. On the early flags, stripes were added as well as stars when new states entered the Union. The real "Star Spangled Banner" had fifteen stripes and fifteen stars. Since then, only stars have been added to symbolize additional states.

Many people have died protecting our country, and the flag reminds many of us of all the great things about America for which people were willing to give their lives. This feeling of love for our country is called "patriotism."

Sometimes people use the flag to protest when they disagree with government actions. They burn the flag, walk on it, or hang it upside down. This has led groups of Americans to fight one another, as each group uses the American flag to symbolize its own beliefs.

The GREAT SEAL *of* THE UNITED STATES

⚜

THE GREAT SEAL IS THE "COAT OF ARMS" OF THE UNITED STATES. It is attached to all important government documents, and it hangs in front of every American embassy in foreign countries. It is the official symbol of our nation. Because of its importance, it wasn't easy for Congress to agree on its design; in fact, it took them twelve years! They started to work on it in 1776, but it wasn't adopted until 1788.

The eagle is probably the first thing you notice on the Seal. It clutches arrows in one of its claws and an olive branch in the other. These symbolize the power of both war and peace. On the eagle's breast is a shield with thirteen vertical stripes, representing the thirteen original states, just as the stripes on the flag do. But the stripes on the shield are reversed from those of the flag. On the flag, there are seven red and six white stripes, but on the eagle's shield, there are six red and seven white stripes. The eagle holds a banner in its beak that reads *E pluribus unum,* meaning "one out of many" in Latin. This refers to the single, united nation made from many states. Over the eagle's head is a crest of thirteen stars breaking through a cloud. These stars represent the constellation of the United States joining the other free powers of the world.

The AMERICAN BALD EAGLE

In 1734, a Creek Indian chief presented feathers from a bald eagle to King George II of England as a sign of everlasting peace between his nation and England. The chief told the king that the eagle represented "the power of the land." Since then, the bald eagle has been our symbol of independence and strength. Actually, eagles have been popular symbols of power since ancient times, and many nations and empires, including the Roman Empire, used the eagle as their official symbol. The eagle appears as part of many other American symbols, such as the Great Seal of the United States, and on coins, paper money, and stamps.

But how would you feel if our national mascot was a turkey instead? Believe it or not, this almost happened! Benjamin Franklin actually thought the turkey would make a good national bird because it was native and unique to North America, but after much debate, the bald eagle was finally chosen in 1782 because of its majestic appearance. The bald eagle's wingspan averages seven to twelve feet; it stands three feet tall and weighs from eight to twelve pounds. The eagle can fly as high as one thousand feet, and its eyesight is so good that it can spot a fish from three miles away!

Not too long ago, however, our national symbol almost became extinct because of hunters and deadly pesticides. By 1970, only about one thousand bald eagles remained in this country. Since then, special efforts have been made to protect this living symbol of America, and there are several thousand bald eagles soaring over the continental United States today. As of May 1998, the bald eagle population had increased enough so that the eagle was removed from the list of endangered species.

The LIBERTY BELL

THE LIBERTY BELL IS FAMOUS FOR ITS CRACK. THE FIRST BELL cracked the first time it was rung, and another bell was cast to replace it. But when this new bell was rung in a funeral procession in 1835, it cracked, too! The crack was patched, but it cracked yet again when the bell was rung in 1846 at a commemoration of George Washington's birthday. The bell hasn't been rung since.

The Liberty Bell was actually known as the "State House Bell" (of Philadelphia) after it was made in England in 1752. During the Revolutionary War, when the British occupied Philadelphia, the bell was taken to nearby Allentown, Pennsylvania, and hidden under the floor of the Zion Reformed Church for safekeeping.

In 1839, the antislavery movement adopted this bell as a symbol of freedom, and from then on, the antislavery activists referred to it as the "Liberty Bell" in their literature. On the hundredth birthday of American independence in 1875, the bell left Philadelphia and went on a tour to many American cities. Then everyone began calling it the Liberty Bell. Inspired by the bell, Americans also began to use the phrase "Let Freedom Ring."

Even though it has stopped ringing, the bell is still a symbol of American independence and liberty. It is on display in Independence Square in Philadelphia for all to see. Inscribed on the bell are the famous words "Proclaim liberty throughout all the land unto all the inhabitants thereof." Through the centuries, the Liberty Bell has guarded three types of freedom: religious freedom for the colonists of Pennsylvania, independence for American colonists, and freedom for American slaves.

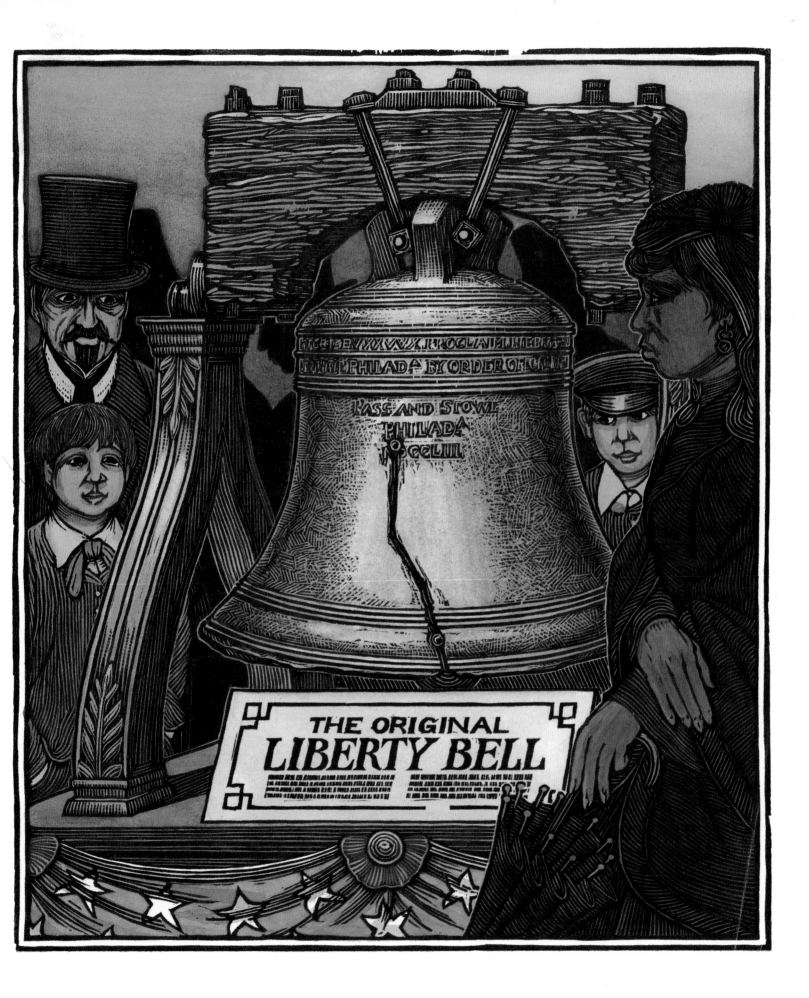

The STATUE OF LIBERTY

⁓✦⁓

With her torch thrust high above the New York City skyline, the Statue of Liberty is, with the exception of the flag, probably the most recognized and powerful symbol of America around the world today. Each year, millions of people ride a ferry from New York City to visit the statue. A spiral staircase leads to the Statue of Liberty's crown, and from there visitors can look out through a row of viewing windows over the waters of New York Harbor, where arriving immigrants from Europe got their first glimpse of the land of freedom.

It is said that the French sculptor Frédéric-Auguste Bartholdi used his mother as the model for the statue's face. The statue was given by France to the United States in 1878 in celebration of their alliance during the American Revolution. "Lady Liberty," as the statue is fondly nicknamed, looks a little green now because she is made of copper, which takes on a greenish tint, called a "patina," as it weathers. She weighs a hefty 225 tons, and her index fingers are eight feet long! Her nose is over four feet long, and her mouth is three feet wide.

She was installed on Bedloe's Island, renamed Liberty Island, in New York City's harbor on October 28, 1886. Her pedestal base was inscribed in 1903 with the now-famous verse by Emma Lazarus that includes these lines:

Give me your tired, your poor,
Your huddled masses yearning to breathe free.

This is a tribute to the millions of immigrants who sailed past Lady Liberty on their way to Ellis Island to enter the United States of America, their new country, full of hope and the promise of freedom.

UNCLE SAM

***

PERHAPS YOU'VE SEEN HIM IN PARADES OR AT A FOURTH OF JULY picnic. He sometimes appears at patriotic gatherings clad in a long blue coat, a vest, and red and white striped trousers. He normally wears a beard and a tall striped and starred hat, and he appears to be dressed to look like the American flag. Who is he? He is "Uncle Sam," a cartoon symbol for the United States of America.

There is much debate about who Uncle Sam was and how the symbol came to be. The first mention of him was in a Troy, New York, newspaper article that appeared on September 7, 1813. It seems that a certain meat-processing plant owner named Sam Wilson began stamping the meat sold to the United States Army during the War of 1812 with the letters "U.S." The meatpackers at his plant called Sam Wilson "Uncle Sam," and the story was that the initials "U.S." really stood for "Uncle Sam" Wilson rather than "United States." The nickname stuck, and from then on everything belonging to the United States government began to be called "Uncle Sam's." Soon, cartoonists latched on to this idea, and they began drawing varieties of Uncle Sam in political cartoons. The most famous depictions of Uncle Sam were on World War I and World War II military recruiting posters. Today, no patriotic gathering would be complete without an appearance by someone dressed as Uncle Sam.

A YANKEE SONG

Yankee Doodle went to town,
  A-riding on a pony,
Stuck a feather in his cap,
  and called it macaroni.

CHORUS:

Yankee Doodle, keep it up,
* Yankee Doodle dandy.*
Mind the music and the step
* and with the girls be handy.*

Father and I went down to camp
  along with Captain Gooding,
And there we saw both men and boys
  as thick as hasty pudding.

CHORUS

There was Captain Washington
  upon a slapping stallion,
Giving orders to his men—
  there must have been a million.

CHORUS

The troopers, they would gallop up
  and fire right in our faces;
It scared me almost half to death
  to see them run such races.

CHORUS

Then I saw a giant gun,
  large as a log of maple,
Upon a very little cart,
  a load for Father's cattle.

CHORUS

And every time they shot it off,
  it took a horn of powder
And made a noise like Father's gun,
  only a nation louder.

CHORUS

I can't tell you but half I saw,
  they kept up such a smother;
I took my hat off, made a bow,
  and scampered home to Mother.

CHORUS

finis

YANKEE DOODLE

EVERY AMERICAN KNOWS THE TUNE TO THIS CATCHY SONG, which isn't surprising, since it has been in existence since colonial times. The origin of the song is unknown, but it was probably composed in the 1750s.

In 1755, a British army officer used the song to make fun of the ragged colonial soldiers from New England who fought with the British against the French and Indians. "Yankee" came from a Dutch nickname for New Englanders, and a "doodle" meant a "foolish person," so in the song the Yankee was a fool. Fashionable people in London wore enormous topknots of hair in a style called "macaroni," and so the British army officer was implying that colonial soldiers were hicks and didn't know anything about fashion, since they thought a feather was macaroni. The song also jokes that Yankees would be so frightened by the loud noises of the cannons that they would run home to their mothers!

Twenty years later, when the colonial soldiers were fighting the British in the Revolutionary War, this song was used again to jeer the colonial army. But this time, colonial soldiers turned the joke around, and, instead of being insulted, made "Yankee Doodle" their song of revolution. They sang it marching into battle, and it was played triumphantly at the victories of Saratoga and Yorktown. "Yankee Doodle" became our first national anthem, and people everywhere began calling all Americans "Yankees."

The MAYFLOWER

⋯✦⋯

Of all the ships that brought settlers to America from England, the *Mayflower* is the most famous. Even today, families boast of their long-standing American heritage by claiming that one of their ancestors came to America on board the *Mayflower* in 1620.

It took about three months for the *Mayflower* to cross the Atlantic. There were approximately 102 passengers aboard the 90-by-26-foot ship, which made for a tight squeeze. About half of the passengers were Pilgrims; the rest were soldiers and other English settlers.

Before the *Mayflower* landed on the shores of what was to become America, the male settlers on board decided to write an agreement to work together and obey all the rules they made as a group. They were convinced that if they didn't cooperate, they would all die in their new colony. This document was called the "Mayflower Compact." Because of the spirit of togetherness on the *Mayflower,* it has become a symbol of cooperation and of the hardy colonial immigrants who tested their courage and faith as they made their place in the New World.

Half of the *Mayflower* colonists died of sickness during their first winter in America. By the time spring arrived, however, the Pilgrims had become friends with a Native American named Squanto, who taught them how to grow corn and to survive in their new land.

The PILGRIM

❧✦❧

WHEN YOU THINK OF A PILGRIM, YOU PROBABLY IMAGINE A PERSON in a funny-looking black hat and black trousers with short leggings and a white shirt with a black tie. Although this has become a popular image, Pilgrims actually dressed the same as other Englishmen of their time.

The Pilgrims were a very small group of early English settlers in the New World colonies. They had broken away from the Church of England because they disagreed with the Church's laws. They came to the New World to be allowed to worship in their own way. The word "pilgrim" means "traveler," and the Pilgrims were given that name by William Bradford, the second governor of the group that settled in the Plymouth Colony. Because of their rebellion from the Church of England, and their difficult adjustment to the New World, Pilgrims represent the hardy early colonial settler and the ideal of religious freedom.

We have the Pilgrims to thank for the Thanksgiving feast we enjoy every year in November. After surviving the harsh first winter in the colony, the Pilgrims learned to live in the wilderness with the help of friendly Native American people. They invited these Native Americans to share a feast they had made from the colony's first harvest. They didn't call the celebration "Thanksgiving," however, but "Harvest Home" after an old English holiday.

Our Thanksgiving meal lasts only one day, but the Pilgrims' feast went on for three! Their menu was similiar to ours today except that there is no record of turkey being served. They feasted on deer, duck, clams and oysters, corn and cornbread, squash, wild berries, beer and wine. And while today we watch football on TV after the Thanksgiving meal, the Pilgrims enjoyed wrestling matches, footraces, tag, and other games.

The PEACE PIPE

SMOKING THE PEACE PIPE WAS PART OF A SOLEMN CEREMONY FOR Native American peoples which guaranteed peace between their nations. After important members of the tribes gathered in a circle, a leader, usually an elder chief, began the ceremony by holding up the stem and bowl of an ancient pipe made from clay and adorned with feathers or beads. He slowly filled the bowl of the pipe, saying a prayer to the great spirits after each pinch of tobacco was added. He would then join the stem to the bowl, singing a sacred song, and place a live coal from the fire over the bowl to light the tobacco. Once it was lit, the leader offered the smoke to the spiritual powers by pointing the pipe north, south, east, and west toward the sky and then toward the earth. He would then pass the pipe to the others in the circle, who each repeated the ritual. Passing the pipe around the circle created a feeling of oneness among the members of the group, and the tobacco smoke drifting upward eased communication with the spirits above.

The peace pipe was not used by all Native American peoples, but many nations practiced this ceremony. The symbolism of the ritual was so powerful that it was recognized by European settlers, and "to smoke the peace pipe" has become a part of our language. Today the peace pipe is an emblem of peaceful relations and cooperation among peoples worldwide.

The MINUTEMAN

⟡

The minuteman is a familiar image of a patriotic colonial soldier standing at attention holding a rifle in his right hand. He is the symbol of the citizen soldier, the key unit in the United States Army and the one upon whom we rely for protection during wars. The term was coined on the eve of the American Revolution, when the revolutionary leaders of Massachusetts set up regiments of men ready to fight "on a minute's notice." Since they were trained to take up arms immediately in an emergency, they were nicknamed "minutemen." Every colonial soldier killed at the first Revolutionary War battle at Lexington, Massachusetts, in April 1775 was a minuteman. Other colonies also organized Minuteman groups, but the formation of a Continental Army limited their use. Unlike some nations where a full-time professional army protects its citizens, American soldiers serve a series of short-term enlistments and have always seen themselves as citizens trained to fight to protect their country. Many men and women have served the United States of America through their state National Guards or through these short-term enlistments in the United States Army, Navy, Air Force, or Marine Corps.

The LOG CABIN

꘡⭐꘡

HAVE YOU EVER PLAYED WITH LINCOLN LOGS? DID YOU KNOW that they are named after President Abraham Lincoln, who was born in a log cabin?

The first settlers to use log cabins were the Swedes and Finns who colonized the Delaware valley around 1638. Log cabins had been built in Scandinavia since about 800 A.D. Later, Early American settlers needed shelter as they moved west across the country, expanding the frontier lands. The building material that was easiest to use was the timber of the trees in the dense forests they encountered on their way. The settlers cut down these trees and quickly erected log houses, which became one of the most popular structures in early America.

Building a log cabin was fairly simple, as settlers needed only one tool: an axe. By notching the ends of logs and laying them horizontally on top of one another, the cabin was held together at the corners and no nails were needed. The builder used clay to fill in the cracks between the logs, and the floor was made of dirt or logs split in half with the flat side facing up.

The log cabin soon became the typical frontier dwelling. It was snug and secure; arrows and bullets could not get through the logs. Gradually, the log cabin became a symbol of the rugged American lifestyle, of people setting out on their own to follow their dreams. Americans gained a deep satisfaction from their ability to conquer the land of an enormous continent, and as they pushed their way west across the frontier, they developed a spirit of pride, confidence, and optimism. The log cabin became such an important symbol that by the mid-1800s, after most Americans had built more elaborate housing, politicians often claimed that they had been "born in a log cabin." They wanted to suggest that they were from humble roots and had a pioneering spirit, which they knew would appeal to American voters.

The BUFFALO

❦★❦

THE BUFFALO AND THE BALD EAGLE ARE FIERCE CONTENDERS FOR the animal symbol of America. To people around the world, the American bison, called a buffalo by the first Europeans to see it, represents America's land and, especially, the history of the American West. Vast herds of buffaloes lived on the western plains at the time of European settlement.

The buffalo was the key to the survival of Native Americans living in the plains area of the western United States. It provided them with all of their basic needs: food, clothing, fuel, shelter, weapons, and utensils. In fact, the buffalo was so important, it came to represent life itself to many Native American nations. But, eventually, new settlers came from the East and wanted the land these native people tradionally held. Knowing how important the buffalo was to Native Americans' survival, the settlers decided that the best way to get the land was to destroy the Plains Indians' way of life by destroying the buffalo. They were so successful that the buffalo population dropped from fifteen million in 1880 to only five hundred in 1885. Today there are buffalo preserves in the United States and Canada to protect this important American symbol in hopes of reintroducing it to the western prairie.

The buffalo makes its most prominent appearance on the seal of the United States Department of the Interior and also on the buffalo nickel. When the buffalo nickel was designed in 1913, the goal was to make it a "true American coin," one that wouldn't be confused with the coin of any other country. The American buffalo was the most distinctive symbol the designers could imagine.

A Plains Indian was featured on the other side of the coin. It is interesting to note that these two symbols of America—the buffalo and the Indian—were only used after both had almost been eradicated from the American scene.

The COWBOY

~★~

A COWBOY SWAGGERS THROUGH THE DOORS OF A DUSTY SALOON in the Old West, his silver spurs spinning on his boots, a revolver on each hip, a mean look on his face. His trusty horse waits outside while he settles some business with another cowboy or two cowering at the bar.

Actually, real cowboys in the nineteenth century weren't called cowboys at all, but "herders" or "vaqueros." The name "cowboy" was created by authors and showmen. A cowboy's days were filled with hard work and long hours at low wages. Cowboys did ride horses, and many carried guns in holsters to protect the herds of cattle they were supposed to guide to water, grazing areas, and market. Cowboys were often wild, rough men, and they had a poor reputation; some of them were actual outlaws.

But then Wild West shows and cheap, popular books called "dime novels" tamed this image of the wild cowboy into an ideal of the American spirit. Cowboys were portrayed as self-sufficient, generous, brave, and honest, with a code of personal honor that made them seem like medieval knights. This image of the "gallant cowboy," familiar today from American books, film, and television, has come to symbolize the ideal American, a self-made man who overcomes his poverty and lack of education with courage, individualism, and determination.

SMOKEY *the* BEAR

"ONLY YOU CAN PREVENT FOREST FIRES!" EVERYONE RECOGNIZES these words as the message of Smokey the Bear. The famous bear wearing his belt and ranger hat was created as a logo in 1944 to prevent the waste caused by forest fires. Since then, Smokey has moved beyond forest fires to become a larger symbol of the American concern for protecting the environment.

Smokey was born when officials in the United States Forest Service decided they wanted to create a symbol to make people more aware of the dangers of forest fires. An artist named Albert Staehle, who worked for the *Saturday Evening Post* magazine, drew a picture of a little bear dressed in a forest ranger's hat and belt. He was named after Smokey Joe Ryan, a famous New York City fire chief of that time.

There was a real Smokey the Bear, too. In 1950, a black bear cub was badly burned in a forest fire in New Mexico and was nursed back to health at a ranger station. When he was better, he was selected to become the first "live" Smokey. He was flown to Washington, D.C., and lived at the National Zoological Park. Today, there is still a living Smokey the Bear at this zoo to remind visitors to show concern for the environment and to help prevent forest fires.

For FURTHER READING

Amato, Carol A. *The Bald Eagle: Free Again!* Hauppauge, NY: Barrons Juveniles, 1996.

Ayer, Eleanor. *Our Flag.* Brookfield, CT: Millbrook Press, 1994.

Bromley, Robin. *The Story of Smokey the Bear.* New York: Penguin, 1996.

Cody, Tod. *The Cowboy's Handbook: How to Become a Hero of the Wild West.*
New York: Dutton, 1996.

Fisher, Leonard E. *Stars and Stripes: Our National Flag.* New York: Holiday House, 1993.

Fisher, Leonard E. *The Statue of Liberty.* New York: Holiday House, 1985.

Giblin, James Cross. *Fireworks, Picnics, and Flags: The Story of the Fourth of July Symbols.*
New York: Clarion, 1983.

Gorsline, Marie and Douglas. *Cowboys.* New York: Random House, 1980.

The Great Seal of the United States. Washington, D.C.: U.S. Government Printing Office, 1996.

Karl, Jean. *America Alive: A History.* New York: Philomel, 1994.

Kellogg, Steven. *Yankee Doodle.* New York: Simon & Schuster, 1976.

Maestro, Betsy. *The Story of the Statue of Liberty.* New York: Morrow, 1986.

McGovern, Ann. *If You Sailed on the Mayflower in 1620.* New York: Scholastic, 1993.

Miller, Robert H. *The Story of Nat Love.* New York: Silver Burdett, 1994.

Patent, Dorothy H. *Eagles of America.* New York: Holiday House, 1995.

Roop, Peter and Connie. *Pilgrim Voices: Our First Year in the New World.*
New York: Walker, 1998.

Rounds, Glen. *The Cowboy Trade.* New York: Holiday House, 1994.

San Souçi, Robert. *N.C. Wyeth's Pilgrims.* San Francisco: Chronicle Books, 1991.

Scott, Ann H. *Cowboy Country.* New York, Clarion, 1993.

Sewall, Marcia. *The Pilgrims of Plimoth.* New York: Atheneum, 1986.

The Smokey the Bear Story. U.S. Forest Service Staff, 1995.

Stone, Lynn M. *Back from the Edge: The American Bison.* Rourke, 1991.

Swanson, Diane. *Buffalo Sunrise: The Story of a Northern American Giant.*
San Francisco: Sierra Club, 1996.

Waters, Kate. *On the Mayflower: Voyages of the Ship's Apprentice & A Passenger Girl.*
New York: Scholastic, 1996.